NEW VANGUARD 247

SOVIET LEND-LEASE TANKS OF WORLD WAR II

STEVEN J. ZALOGA   ILLUSTRATED BY HENRY MORSHEAD

First published in Great Britain in 2017 by Osprey Publishing,
PO Box 883, Oxford, OX1 9PL, UK
1385 Broadway, 5th Floor, New York, NY 10018, USA
E-mail: info@ospreypublishing.com

Osprey Publishing, part of Bloomsbury Publishing Plc

A CIP catalogue record for this book is available from the British Library

Print ISBN: 978 1 4728 1813 3
PDF e-book ISBN: 978 1 4728 1814 0
ePub e-book ISBN: 978 1 4728 1815 7
XML ISBN: 978 1 4728 2717 3

Index by Alan Rutter
Typeset in Sabon and Myriad Pro
Originated by PDQ Media, Bungay, UK
Printed in China through World Print Ltd.

17 18 19 20 21 10 9 8 7 6 5 4 3 2 1

Osprey Publishing supports the Woodland Trust, the UK's leading woodland
conservation charity. Between 2014 and 2018 our donations are being
spent on their Centenary Woods project in the UK.

To find out more about our authors and books visit
www.ospreypublishing.com. Here you will find extracts, author
interviews, details of forthcoming events and the option to sign up for
our newsletter.

AUTHOR'S NOTE

The author would especially like to thank Joe Demarco and Viktor Kulikov
for help on this project.

CONTENTS

SOVIET LEND-LEASE TANKS OF WORLD WAR II

INTRODUCTION

During World War II, the United States, Britain and Canada provided the Red Army with about 11,660 tanks, equivalent to about 13 percent of Soviet tank production. These weapons were commonly called "Lend-Lease," though this term in fact refers specifically to the American program, however, the term is used here for the sake of convenience. The Lend-Lease tanks have remained a controversial subject. During the Communist era, these weapons were usually deprecated as too few in number and of poor quality, whereas Western accounts have often depicted Lend-Lease as a "lifesaver" for the Soviet Union.

THE EARLY SHIPMENTS

A column of M3S tanks of the 193rd Separate Tank Regiment which served with the 48th Army on the Central Front on the northern side of the Kursk salient in the July 1943 battles. The regiment was formed at the Gorkiy tank school in October 1942 and initially had 39 M3S tanks.

Germany invaded its erstwhile ally, the Soviet Union, on June 22, 1941. Overnight, Moscow went from being an enemy of Britain to an ally. Churchill famously said that "if Hitler invaded Hell, I would make at least a favourable reference to the Devil in the House of Commons," and after decades as one of Britain's most ardent anti-Communists, Churchill vowed to assist the Soviet Union in their common struggle against Hitler. Churchill realized that Britain was no longer alone in its struggle with Germany and that the German invasion of the Soviet Union offered Britain temporary salvation from any German cross-Channel onslaught. The British–Soviet alliance was a matter of convenience not trust. Lt Gen Henry Pownall, vice-chief of the Imperial General Staff, offered a more pungent view in his diary at the time, a view that was widely shared within the upper echelons of the British Army: "I avoid the expression 'Allies' for the Russians are a dirty lot of murdering thieves themselves, and double crossers of the deepest dye. It is good to see the two biggest cut-throats in Europe, Hitler and Stalin, going for each other."

The British tanks first went into combat with the Red Army during the battles on the approaches to Moscow in November–December 1941, including both the MK.2 (Matilda) as seen here and MK.3 (Valentine).

By mid-July, Stalin was demanding that Britain open a "Second Front" in Europe, an operation far beyond Britain's capabilities at that time. Stalin had a very poor understanding of British military forces, and at one point suggested a preposterous scheme for Britain to dispatch an expeditionary force of 20 divisions to land at Arkhangelsk and conduct the war from Soviet soil. Instead, Churchill offered military aid as a palliative. In late June 1941 Moscow had sent Britain a list of its requirements, which included 3,000 fighters, 3,000 bombers and numerous other items. British tanks were not high on the list.

The British armed forces suffered from their own shortages of equipment, and any aid sent to Moscow would have to come at the expense of Britain's own requirements. Churchill later noted that "in order to make this immense diversion (to the USSR) without crippling our campaign in the Western Desert, we had to cramp all our preparations which prudence urged for the defence of the Malay peninsula and our Eastern Empire and possessions against the ever growing menace of Japan." In the wake of the loss of Singapore, foreign minister Anthony Eden in January 1942 remarked that "The simple truth was that we had given to Russia what we ourselves needed here and now and that in consequence we had not really got enough for ourselves."

Due to its own shortages, Britain was beginning to receive American weapons under Franklin Roosevelt's "Lend-Lease" program. This effort had been started in March 1941 as a method to support Britain in the face of the isolationist popular sentiment in the United States. In late July 1941, Churchill proposed diverting some Lend-Lease fighters to the Soviet Union due to the shortage of suitable British fighters. As in Britain, the American military leadership was deeply suspicious of the Soviet Union even though President Roosevelt, in late July 1941, promised Moscow substantial military aid.

In August 1941, Moscow began to show interest in receiving tanks. During an impromptu visit to Moscow by one of Roosevelt's close aides, Harry Hopkins, Stalin indicated he would like to send Soviet specialists with tank designs to manufacture them in the United States. This proposal was ignored rather than rejected and the Soviets never pressed the idea any further. Hopkins, the Secretary of Commerce, was the key US official in overseeing Lend-Lease. His British counterpart was Lord Beaverbrook and their Soviet contact was Anastas Mikoyan.

Due to the military disasters in the summer of 1941 and the heavy Soviet tank losses, Moscow's attitude toward a supply of tanks from Britain and the United States underwent a dramatic change. In the autumn of 1941, Moscow demanded 1,100 tanks per month; British tank production in 1941 totaled 4,834 and the United States produced 4,052, for a combined average of 740 monthly, so Britain and the United States agreed to a tentative objective of supplying the Soviet Union with 500 tanks per month, as well as 200 Universal Carriers, based largely on the presumption that 1942 tank production would substantially exceed 1941 production. These objectives were contained in the "First Protocol" which covered October 1941 to June 1942.

The Soviet demands were essentially those of a bankrupt millionaire turning to a pauper for salvation. The Red Army had started the war with nearly 23,000 tanks but promptly lost nearly 12,000 of its best ones in the first three weeks of the war. By the end of 1941, it had lost 20,500 tanks, a force many times the size of the combined British and American tank parks. To put this in some perspective, the British Army had about 1,770 tanks in front-line service in June 1941 of which 780 were in North Africa. To meet the Soviet tank demands, Britain diverted its own infantry tank production to the Red Army, and in turn pressured the US to increase Lend-Lease medium tank transfers to British forces in the Middle East, slowing the formation of the US armored divisions. These pressures were greatest in late 1941 through 1942 when British and American production was still growing; the pressures abated in 1943 once American tank production reached its peak.

INITIAL BRITISH SHIPMENTS

A special Soviet liaison mission arrived in Britain in the autumn of 1941 to learn about the types of tanks available. They rejected British cruiser tanks as being not much different than the Soviet BT-7 and showed no interest in the MK.VI light tank. They finally settled on the two British infantry tanks, the Matilda and Valentine.

The first British tank deliveries in 1941 were conducted via Arctic convoys to the port of Arkhangelsk, which soon became a dangerous delivery method due to U-boat and aircraft attack on the convoys. The first convoy with 20 Valentine tanks, PQ.1, arrived at Arkhangelsk on October 11, 1941. The tanks were shipped with the equivalent of three months of ammunition, typically 640 2-pdr rounds and 17,300 Besa machine-gun rounds, along with associated small arms such as Bren guns and Thompson SMG. Of the 750 tanks promised under the protocols for 1941, Britain shipped 259 Valentine and 145 Matilda infantry tanks. At least one document indicates that "a few M3 light cruisers" (Stuarts) were sent in convoy PQ.2A. Russian sources indicate 216 Valentines and 145 Matildas arriving, but there are discrepancies between British and Soviet records due to dates of convoy departure versus arrival, as well as losses of ships due to German attacks. There were no US Lend-Lease tank deliveries in 1941 according to US records.

On October 15, 1941, the Red Army established a special course at the Kazan tank school to train Soviet tank crews on British tanks and the first 20 Valentines from PQ.1 arrived there on October 28, 1941. A second school was subsequently established near Gorkiy (now Nizhni-Novgorod). British tankers sent to Kazan to assist in training described the Soviet crews as "very keen, appear experienced, and quality of rank and file compares favorably to the British pre-war tank standards … They are all well satisfied with our tanks except for points noted." On the other hand, the British instructors had a hard time teaching British gunnery practices due to the Soviet officers preferring Soviet practices; the crews were reluctant to use the power traverse and insisted on manual traverse. The Soviet crews were inherently averse to learning to use the internal communication system or wireless set and preferred to use Soviet methods such as visual signals. The quality of the new crews varied. Although the first cadre was already well trained, subsequent batches were woefully unprepared, and it proved difficult to get them ready in the limited 15-day course.

By late November 1941, the Red Army had formed six tank battalions including 20 Matildas and 97 Valentines. These were deployed mainly on the Western Front in the defense of Moscow. The first unit deployed with British tanks was the 146th Tank Brigade (146-*ya tankovaya brigada*) of the 16th Army consisting of two tank battalions with a total of 40 Valentines and two Matildas. The first unit to receive the Matilda was the 136th Separate Tank Battalion (136-*y otdelniy tankoviy batal'on*) which was equipped with 20 tanks in November 1941. The Red Army usually referred to the Matilda as the MK.2 and the Valentine as the MK.3 regardless of which production batch was involved. This sometimes led to confusion. For example, some recent Russian accounts have suggested that the US supplied some

A Matilda tank named "Tank chetyrem geroyev" (Tank of Four Heroes), commanded by Sr Lt G. N. Fokin on the left, and next to him, the company commander, Capt A. I. Voytov of the 182nd Separate Tank Battalion, 202nd Tank Brigade, 19th Tank Corps, seen on the Central Front in January 1943. This is apparently the same Fokin who was awarded the "Hero of the Soviet Union" decoration in November 1942 for his exploits as a KV-1 tank platoon commander with the 6th Tank Brigade, credited with destroying 16 German tanks in May 1942.

A Valentine II knocked out during the fighting in southern Russia in the summer of 1942. It still has its shipping instructions to Arkhangelsk painted on the mudguards.

M2 medium tanks which was not the case; it was simply a typographical error substituting M2 for MK.2.

The Lend-Lease tanks played an unusually prominent role in the defense of Moscow due to the relatively small size of the Soviet tank force as a result of the summer military disasters. In November 1941 there were about 670 tanks in the fronts defending Moscow, and in December 1941 there were 607, of which only 205 were the T-34 medium tank and KV heavy tank – the remainder were various types of light tanks. Historian Alexander Hill has argued that the British tanks constituted 30–40 percent of the medium and heavy tanks in the defense of Moscow, but Russian historians have retorted that the Red Army considered the Valentine and Matilda to be light tanks. Actually, they fell in between Soviet light and medium tanks, having less firepower than Soviet medium and heavy tanks, but better armor than Soviet light tanks. They were certainly better than the dreadful Soviet T-60 light tank, the most common tank type in production in late 1941 to early 1942 next to the T-34 medium tank. The Matilda had armor similar to that of the KV-1 heavy tank.

Regardless of this argument, the combat debut of the British tanks came at a critical time for the Red Army. By late December 1941, some 182 British tanks had been committed to combat, of which 77 had been lost. By late December, there were only 46 Lend-Lease tanks in service with the Western Front, eight Matildas and 38 Valentines. Following the Moscow battles, many of these units were pulled out of the line to wait for better weather due to the tanks' shortcomings in snow. The defensive battles around Moscow had been very costly for the Soviet tank force, and on January 1, 1942, the Western Front had a mere 47 tanks operational of which 15 were Valentines.

The newcomers proved ill-suited to Russian winter weather. British tanks had been designed to operate down to 0 degrees C but temperatures down to -50 degrees C were not uncommon in Russia in winter. Of the two British tanks, the Valentine was preferred. The Matilda's tracks had poor traction on the snow, and the enclosed suspension tended to become clogged with compacted snow. Most Matildas delivered to the Soviet Union used the simple T.D.5910 "spud" tracks which were flat tractor-style tracks with poor

 A

1: MATILDA, 136TH SEPARATE TANK BATTALION, MOSCOW AREA, DECEMBER 1941

The early British tanks provided to the Red Army came in their original G3 Khaki Green camouflage paint. Before being committed to the fighting in November 1941, they were usually over-painted with white-wash as seen here. This often consisted of expedient paint such as a solution of lime, so it tended to wear off, exposing the base green color underneath.

2: MATILDA, 7TH TANK BRIGADE, SOUTHWEST FRONT, MAY 1942

This Matilda was also painted in the G3 Khaki Green camouflage paint. There had been complaints from the Russians about tanks being shipped via the Arctic route without antifreeze in the radiators. As a result, tanks in later shipments had an antifreeze mixture, and this was clearly marked in both Russian and English on the hull side. Instructions were also added regarding the fording flaps. The "T" number is the normal British census number that was often left on the tanks for paper-keeping even in the Red Army units. Soviet tactical markings during this period were peculiar to local units and were intended to frustrate German intelligence collection. The camouflage on the turret is daubed mud.

1

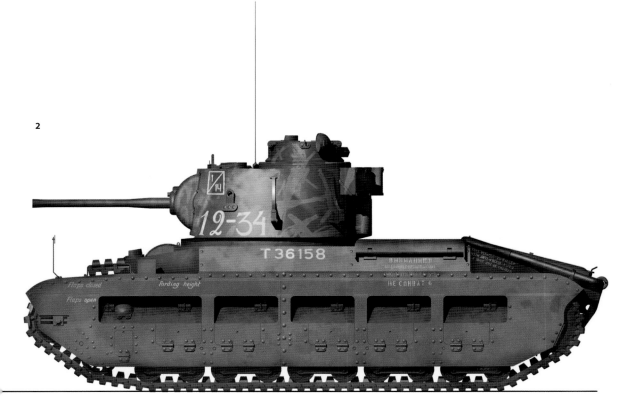

2

performance in snow. The Red Army units found that 30cm (12 inches) of snow would stop a Matilda. The Matilda was also unusually slow by Soviet standards, and the two-engine configuration was a maintenance burden. On the other hand, the armor protection on the Matilda was prized since it was comparable to the KV heavy tank. One Soviet tanker reported his tank had been hit 87 times without penetration. The Valentine was faster, and the suspension was viewed as more durable and functional in cross-country travel. Its tracks were far from perfect, but better than the Matilda's in the snow. The main complaints about the Valentine were the engine deck configuration which the Soviet troops thought was needlessly vulnerable, and the position of the exhaust which blinded the driver when starting.

Churchill had directed the Minister of Supply, Lord Beaverbrook, to manage the British program of aid to the Soviet Union. On December 3, 1941, Beaverbrook received a personal message from Stalin that urged Britain to increase the number of Valentines and decrease the number of Matildas due to the Valentine's superior performance in winter weather. Beaverbrook agreed to do so, but in view of the limited industrial resources and Britain's own armament needs, Matildas continued to be shipped through 1942.

The most substantial tactical deficit with both the Valentine and Matilda was their 2-pdr gun. Although it had antiarmor capability similar to the standard Soviet 45mm gun, it lacked a high-explosive round. This was a severe drawback since the majority of tank combat involved fighting against enemy troops and antitank guns where high-explosive was essential. The Red Army was so unimpressed with the 2-pdr that it requested that Britain halt the shipment of the towed 2-pdr antitank guns since they did not meet Soviet requirements in the "ballistic properties, penetration and manufacturing quality."

The problems with the 2-pdr led to a crash program to re-arm the tanks. In December 1941, the NKO (People's Defense Committee) ordered the Grabin design bureau at Plant No. 92 in Gorkiy to adapt the ZiS-5 76mm tank gun as used on the KV tank to the Matilda under the designation F-96 (or ZiS-96). This was successful enough that, in January 1942, the government decided to re-equip all Matildas with the F-96 gun. Manufacture began at Plant No. 92 in March 1942, but only 47 of the 120 guns that were ordered that month were actually delivered. There is little evidence that any Matildas beyond the prototype were fitted with 76mm guns or actually issued to the troops. There is at least one German intelligence report that the newly formed 36th and 37th Tank Brigades each had a company of Matildas with 76mm guns, but this has not been confirmed. Britain eventually supplied 156 of the Matilda CS (close support), armed with a 3in gun, but only 125 arrived and they were never very common.

In the case of the Valentine, the turret was too small to accommodate the 76mm gun so Grabin's design bureau was instructed to develop a mounting for the standard 45mm 20-K tank gun, called F-95 in this configuration. Although the mounting proved perfectly functional, the program was abruptly canceled in January 1942 since the 45mm gun didn't offer any better antitank performance and there was a shortage of 45mm guns. Another alternative was to develop a high-explosive round for the gun. One method involved the use of 40mm Bofors high-explosive rounds, remounted on 2-pdr casings. This does not appear to have proceeded beyond tests.

THE CANADIAN VALENTINE

Soviet preference for the Valentine also prompted the decision by the British government to direct nearly all of Canadian production to the Soviet Union. Britain had placed an initial order for 300 Valentine tanks in 1940 along with a Canadian army order for 488 tanks. These were assembled at the Canadian Pacific Railway's Angus Shops in Montreal. The first pilot was completed in May 1941 and the first 30 pre-series tanks were delivered to the Canadian army in the summer of 1941. In October 1941, Britain increased the order with a contract for 1,390 and Canada canceled the remainder of its previous order, substituting other types for its new tank units. Two of the tanks from this contract remained in Britain for trials purposes. The first shipment of Canadian Valentine VIIs left the Montreal plant in November 1941 but did not arrive in the Soviet Union until 1942. The Canadian-built Valentines were an immediate success in the Soviet Union because the General Motors 6-71 engine was regarded as more reliable than previous British power-plants; it was later adopted on the British-manufactured Valentine IV. A total of 773 Canadian Valentines went to the Soviet Union in 1942 and 615 in 1943. Of the 1,420 Canadian Valentines manufactured through May 1943, 1,388 were sent to the Soviet Union, of which 1,208 arrived.

In late 1942, Vickers began to manufacture the Valentine IX which had an enlarged turret with a 6-pdr gun and two-man crew. To fit in the larger gun, the co-axial machine gun had to be deleted, leaving the tank without secondary armament. Yet this was a significant step forward in firepower and quickly won the approval of the Red Army. Soviet light tanks of this time, notably the T-70 light tank, were still armed with the 45mm gun that was similar to the British 2-pdr in performance. During deliberations over

A Canadian Valentine VII of the 151st Tank Brigade, part of the Black Sea Group of the Caucasus Front, knocked out in the January 1943 fighting. It can be identified as a Canadian-produced tank by the cast nose and the Browning co-axial machine gun.

the "Third Protocol" that covered British shipments from July 1943 to June 1944, British officials were mystified when Soviet officers in London continued to ask for more Valentines versus newer types such as the Cromwell. The War Office in April 1943 remarked that "It is not known why the Russians appear so eager to get Valentines, even when armed with only a 2-pdr gun. It is of course a very reliable tank but cannot be considered a modern weapon." The Director of Armoured Fighting Vehicles was even more blunt, commenting that "though it has done good work, [the Valentine] is now definitely obsolete. Everything that shoots goes through its armour and its 2-pdr is effective neither as an anti-tank nor as an anti-personnel weapon. The 6-pdr Valentine is a bastard, having no machine gun." Production of the Valentine continued into 1943 only to satisfy Soviet requirements.

A total of 927 Valentine IX and Valentine X tanks with 6-pdrs were received by the Red Army in 1943–44. The Valentine was successful enough in Soviet service that the Red Army finally ended its own light tank production in 1943, using the continuing supply of Valentines for its light scout tank needs. Once Soviet production of the T-70 and T-80 tanks ended, the industrial capacity was switched to the SU-76 assault gun. This was based on the hull of the T-70 light tank, but fitted with an open casemate at the rear with the standard 76mm divisional gun. The SU-76M served as the principal infantry close-support vehicle in the Red Army, being built in larger numbers than any other armored fighting vehicle (AFV) except for the T-34 tank. As a result, the Valentine remained in Red Army service through the end of the war in 1945, and even saw combat in the Far East in August 1945 against Japan.

THE TETRARCH LIGHT TANK

The third British tank type to arrive was the Tetrarch airborne tank. A batch of 20 tanks arrived at Zanjan, Iran on the Soviet border on December 27, 1941 and they were finally transferred to Azerbaijan in January 1942.

B

1: VALENTINE VII, 151ST TANK BRIGADE, BLACK SEA GROUP, CAUCASUS FRONT, CRIMEA, JANUARY 1943

In late 1941, the British Army instructed tank plants to switch from the G3 Khaki Green to the SCC No. 2 Brown once existing stockpiles of the previous paint had been exhausted. The switch was due to shortages of chromium oxide (green) pigment. The Canadian plants manufacturing tanks under British contracts followed suit. Details of the meaning of the tactical marking are not known.

2: VALENTINE IX, 5TH GUARDS TANK ARMY, 2ND UKRAINIAN FRONT, AUSTRIA, APRIL 1945

The SCC No. 2 Brown color remained in use as a base color on British tanks through early 1944 when it shifted to SCC No. 15, a British equivalent of US Army olive drab. This tank, built in 1943, remained in the SCC No. 2 color. The white vertical band in front of the tactical number 122 is probably from an air identification band painted on the roof, a common Soviet practice to prevent friendly aircraft from attacking their own tanks.

1

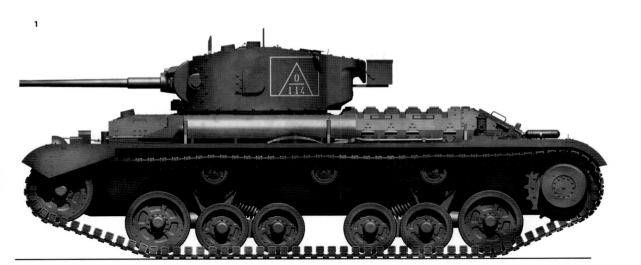

2

One of the rarest Lend-Lease tanks that saw combat with the Red Army was the Tetrarch airborne tank. Twenty of these were delivered to the 21st Separate Tank Training Regiment near Yerevan, Armenia in March 1942 when this staged shot was probably taken. They later served in the Caucasus campaign with the 151st Tank Brigade.

It took time for instructional material to arrive and they were deployed with the 21st Separate Tank Training Regiment near Yerevan, Armenia in March 1942. After spending time on border patrol, the Tetrarchs were deployed with the 151st Tank Brigade alongside T-26 light tanks and sent into combat in January 1943 with the 47th Army of the Trans-Caucasus Front. They were used mainly in infantry support missions and, in March 1943, the brigade was re-equipped. There were still ten Tetrarchs operational plus one that had been sent to Kubinka for evaluation. The ten functional tanks were deployed with the 563rd Separate Tank Brigade that took part in an unsuccessful amphibious landing at Novorossiysk. After this operation, they were handed down to other units but do not appear to have seen further combat. Four broken-down tanks were sent to the 3rd Rifle Corps which emplaced them as static defenses at the Shapsugkiy bridge.

THE LEND-LEASE PROCESS

The military aid program to the Soviet Union was managed through a series of "Protocols" that were negotiated between the three governments to manage the provision of weapons and supplies to the Soviet Union. These negotiations were complicated by the fact that the majority of US Lend-Lease aid was directed to Britain, and there was often a "circle-within-a-circle" with the British negotiating for their share of the American Lend-Lease "pie" prior to arranging allotments for the Soviet Union. For example, the US negotiators to the First Protocol talks had planned to offer the Red Army 795 medium tanks by June 30, 1942, but this would have cut the British allotment to only 611, which London regarded as completely unacceptable. In the event, against the Soviet request for 1,100 tanks per month, Britain and the US offered 2,250 each by the end of June 1942 or 500 per month.

Tank Commitments to the USSR under Military Aid Protocols 1941–45			
		Britain	US
First Protocol	October 1941–30 June 1942	2,250	2,250
Second Protocol	1 July 1942–30 June 1943	3,000	7,000
Third Protocol	1 July 1943–30 June 1944	3,000 (revised:1,000)	0 (revised: 2,000)
Fourth Protocol	1 July 1944–30 June 1945	0	3,000

Of the 4,500 tanks promised under the First Protocol, Britain and the US made available 4,732 of which 4,161 were shipped, but 740 of these were sunk, leaving a final delivery total of 3,421; some 531 more British tanks were en route at the end of the delivery period. Delivery proved to be a major obstacle to fulfilling the early tank program. During 1941, the only delivery route was by means of Arctic convoys to Arkhangelsk and Murmansk in northern Russia. The 1941 deliveries did not face German opposition; however, the Germans quickly caught wind of the scheme and began attacking the Arctic convoys using aircraft, warships, and submarines. The loss of the first merchantman occurred in January 1942 from convoy PQ.7a. The worst of these attacks befell convoy PQ.17 in June 1942 when 22 of its 33 ships were sunk. Convoys were called off for two months as the situation was re-assessed, badly impacting the 1942 Second Protocol deliveries.

Curiously enough, the first joint British–Soviet military action in World War II was Operation *Countenance*, a joint invasion of Iran that started on August 25, 1941. The invasion was intended to prevent Iranian oil from falling into German hands, but also to secure a means for Britain to transport war supplies to the Soviet Union. As Arctic convoy losses grew, more and more effort was put into opening the Persian Gulf corridor. This was a significant engineering feat since there were neither the ports nor land routes available in 1941 to support such a major logistics venture. Another conceivable route was via the Soviet Pacific port of Vladivostok. This did not become practical until 1943 when the Japanese were pushed back out of the Aleutians.

INITIAL US TANK DELIVERIES: M3 LIGHT TANK

The first American tank type delivered was the M3 light tank, popularly called the Stuart in British service. An initial agreement between the US and Soviet government was reached in October 1941 for the delivery of the first batch of 94 M3 light tanks which had been set aside from the

An M3L of the 196th Tank Brigade on the Kalinskiy Front during the winter of 1942–43 with a Matilda evident behind. The tank in the right foreground is from the second production series with the D38976 welded turret manufactured in the summer of 1941.

An M3L of the 241st Tank Brigade on the Don Front in September 1942 with the name "Suvorov" on the hull side and the slogan "Slomim fashistov" (Crush the Fascists) on the turret side. This particular tank is from the later M3 series manufactured in early 1942 with the interim D58101 turret, but without a turret basket, and still with the riveted hull and sponson machine guns.

September and October 1941 acceptance batches. The initial 31 M3 light tanks arrived on convoy PQ.6 which reached Murmansk on December 20, 1941. It is worth noting that US documents do not list any tank deliveries to the Soviet Union in 1941, so either these tanks came from British stocks or they were considered "delivered" only after Soviet government acceptance in January 1942. Some Soviet documents referred to these as M2A4 light tanks, but they were in fact M3 light tanks. These were sent to the training school at Gorkiy. A further 201 followed on PQ.15 that arrived on May 5, 1942, 147 on PQ.16 on May 29 and 39 tanks with the ill-fated PQ.17 on July 10. As a result of the heavy losses suffered by PQ.17, greater efforts were made to open up the land routes through Iran. The first 102 M3 light tanks through Iran arrived in September 1942 and there was a total of 298 in 1942 through this route. In Soviet service, the M3 light tank was designated as the M3L (L= *legkhiy*: light) to distinguish it from the M3 medium tank which was called the M3S (S= *sredniy*: medium). It was first put into action in the spring of 1942 in the fighting in the Kharkov area.

In May 1942, the Commissar of the Tank Industry, Vyacheslav Malyshev, recommended against acquiring more American tanks, based largely on initial test results from the NIIBT Poligon (*Nauchno-ispytatelniy institut bronetankoviy*: Proving ground of the Armor Research-Experimental Institute) at Kubinka near Moscow. The reports complained that they were vulnerable to Molotov cocktails and the flat rubber tracks were deemed to slip too easily on varied ground conditions. Instead Malyshev recommended acquiring more American trucks.

An evaluation by the commander of the armored forces on the Southwestern Front, Gen-Lt Vladimir S. Tamruchi, offered a more balanced assessment based on actual combat experiences. In a June 1942 report

1: M3L, 417TH TANK BATTALION, 192ND TANK BRIGADE, 61ST ARMY, WESTERN FRONT, NORTH OF VOLKHOV, JULY 1942

This unit was formed at the Gorkiy tank center in February 1942 based around Lend-Lease equipment. It included two tank battalions, the 416th and 417th. The brigade at the time included 14 M3S medium tanks, 31 M3L light tanks, two Matildas and a few KV-1 heavy tanks. The unit was decimated during the fighting near Volkhov, losing 24 of its 31 M3L tanks. This tank is finished in overall lusterless olive drab and carries the large four-digit tactical numbers seen on the tanks of this brigade. The first digit indicates the battalion (417th Tank Battalion).

2: M3L, 563RD SEPARATE TANK BATTALION, NORTH CAUCASUS FRONT, YUZHNOY OZEREYKI, FEBRUARY 1943

On the night of February 3/4, 1943, Soviet forces staged amphibious landings on either side of the Black Sea port of Novorossiysk. The amphibious landing at Ozereika Bay included an attempted landing by 33 M3L tanks of the 563rd Separate Tank Battalion. Half the tanks were trapped when their barge was hit by German artillery fire, preventing them from landing. Others were dropped in deep water and their engines were flooded. About a dozen made it to shore, several fighting their way into the nearby towns. The attack was crushed by German coastal artillery fire and over a thousand Soviet infantry and tankers were captured or killed. It was a disaster similar to the ill-fated Dieppe raid of 1942. This M3A1 was part of the force and was painted in the original US Army lusterless olive drab with a Soviet tactical insignia on the hull side.

1

2

The Red Army received some of the improved M3A1 light tanks in the final deliveries. These can be distinguished by the later D58133 turret with turret basket. This version can be distinguished externally by the welded hull and the factory covers over the former location for the sponson machine guns. This particular tank went through testing at the NIIBT Poligon at Kubinka.

Five M5A1 light tanks were delivered to the Soviet Union in 1943 but, by this stage, the Red Army had no interest in these tanks and preferred to receive more Shermans. This is an example at the NIIBT Poligon at Kubinka with the shipping label "TTD" (Toledo Tank Depot) still evident on the side of the turret.

to GABTU (Main Automotive and Tank Administration), he praised the tank for good maneuverability and handling. He felt that the 37mm gun had better performance than either the Soviet 45mm gun or the British 2-pdr, that the track problem was exaggerated and that the American tanks offered quieter travel in dry conditions than comparable metal-tracked tanks. However, they did have traction problems in mud. Tamruchi thought the design was too high and narrow, and so prone to roll-over on slopes. An interesting point made in the report was that the numerous rubber pads inside the tank for crew safety were in fact a fire hazard if the tank began to burn, and it became Soviet practice to remove this material. In general, the M3L was better suited to fast mobile operations due to its speed and handling, and less suited to close infantry support due to its weak armor.

It should be noted that Soviet evaluations of Lend-Lease tanks were all over the map. One report would praise some technical feature only to have a report from another unit damn the same feature. American and British tank personnel at the tank training centers found that the senior commanders tended to be more confident and offered more useful comments, while the junior commanders tended to parrot the anti-foreign rhetoric that had been common in the Soviet Union for decades, and to find fault with everything foreign. As in the case of the Matilda and Valentine, at this point in time the M3L was superior to the contemporary Soviet T-60 light tank, as well as the improved T-70 light tank that began to appear in service later in 1942 as the replacement for the T-60.

The improved M3A1 light tank began arriving in late 1942. These introduced a re-designed turret with a turret basket. Tests at the Kubinka proving ground were critical of the new version, since the turret became extremely cramped due to the new turret basket. It's worth mentioning that the British Army felt the same way, and both armies preferred the earlier versions. In the event, about 340 M3A1 light tanks arrived by April 1943 in the final US Lend-Lease deliveries of this type. A few M5A1 light tanks were also shipped to the Soviet Union, but the Red Army had no interest in this type.

THE M3 MEDIUM TANK

The first M3 (Lee) medium tanks were set aside from the October 1941 acceptance batches and small numbers began arriving in the Soviet Union in early 1942. The Red Army was a bit perplexed by the tank which, as mentioned before, was called M3S to distinguish it from the M3 light tank. The combination of a sponson-mounted 75mm gun and a turreted 37mm gun was very odd,

a view that was shared by many US tankers. The first known deployment of the M3S was with the 114th Tank Brigade on the Southern Front, which on May 20, 1942 had two Matildas, two M3Ss and 21 T-60 light tanks.

One of the first M3Ss that had arrived on February 2, 1942 was sent to Kubinka for trials. The report concluded that "Both the size and design of the hull are not modern. The tank is too tall, and the vertical armor plates with the exception of the front give the tank poor protection from gun fire." The report went on to comment favorably on technical aspects of the tank such as gun layout, engine, and track. One of the odder recommendations of the report was that the large size of the hull permitted the M3S to carry up to ten sub-machine gunners even with the normal seven-man crew in place. The tests found that they could disembark from the large side doors in 25–30 seconds. The M3S was clearly inferior to the T-34 tank in terms of armor. However, the T-34 in 1942 suffered from a rapid decline in factory quality that led to frequent mechanical breakdowns. The M3S was more durable and reliable. In terms of firepower, the performance of the 75mm gun on the M3S was hindered during its first months in combat in the Soviet Union due to the provision of poor quality ammunition. This situation was eventually rectified, giving the M3S somewhat better firepower than the T-34 if only due to the absurd plethora of weapons. The Soviet crews were especially baffled by the twin machine guns in the hull front that were supposed to be aimed by the driver. Although this feature was mocked in 1942, the Red Army itself in 1944–46 adopted a similar weapon on the T-44 and T-54.

As with other American tanks, the rubber-block tracks posed problems in the winter months as they were prone to skidding and sliding on frozen ground. Soviet crews adopted expedient measures such as embedding bolts in the rubber block. The same problem was well known to British and American Sherman crews, and the solution was the use of track grousers or the special metal tracks with integral grousers which were already in the pipeline.

Although there has been speculation that some of the M3Ss sent to the Soviet Union were the diesel-powered sub-variants, recently uncovered documents indicate that all were the standard M3 medium tank with the

A column of M3S tanks of the 153rd Separate Tank Brigade of the 5th Army pass through Vyazma on March 13, 1943. When formed in the summer of 1942, this unit had 24 M3S and 27 M3L tanks.

A total of 130 M31 tank recovery vehicles, based on the M3 medium tank, were supplied to the Soviet Union. This is an M31B1 that served with the Polish LWP's (*Ludowe Wojsko Polskie*: Polish People's Army) 24th Tank Repair Battalion (*Batalion naprawy czołgów*) in 1944–45.

Continental radial engine. Aside from the basic tank version, the M31 tank recovery vehicle was also delivered in modest numbers. Curiously enough, some of these were the diesel-powered versions such as the M31B1.

In spite of frequent Soviet complaints about the M3S, there were still tanks in the pipeline, and they continued to be shipped to the Soviet Union through the first half of 1943. While the Red Army claimed the M3S was obsolete in 1943, it was still in US Army service at this time as well. The US Army used the M3 medium tank in the early tank battles in Tunisia in December 1942 to January 1943. The 1st Armored Division was replenished with M3 medium tanks after the Kasserine Pass defeat in February 1943 since so many of the Shermans had been shipped via Lend-Lease to Britain. US separate tank battalions in Tunisia also operated the M3 medium tank. The last known American use of the M3 medium tank was in 1944 in the Pacific. Interestingly, there was still a single Soviet M3S tank in service during the Operation *August Storm* campaign against Japan in August 1945. In a flourish of rhetorical excess, Soviet propaganda referred to the M3S as the "Grave for Seven Brothers." Once again it is all a matter of perspective. The M3S was inferior to the T-34 in many respects, but it was also markedly superior to many Soviet tanks of the period, especially the wretched T-60 and T-70 light tanks which were still numerous in the summer of 1943.

D **M3S MEDIUM TANKS, 416TH TANK BATTALION, 192ND TANK BRIGADE, 61ST ARMY, WESTERN FRONT, NORTH OF VOLKHOV, JULY 1942**

These two M3S tanks were part of the 192nd Tank Brigade. The brigade was committed to action on the Western Front in the summer of 1942 and took heavy losses in the battles around Volkhov against Panzer-Regiment.35 and German antitank guns. The tanks are still in their overall delivery finish of US Army lusterless olive drab. These tanks carry elaborate patriotic slogans on the front. The tank to the left is named "Soviet Heroes" with the star of the Hero of the Soviet Union below. The tank to the right carries the slogan "Revenge the tortured Soviet People." The side view shows the latter tank, with the tactical number 6121 painted over and so obscuring the US Army registration number W.30x.xxx in blue drab below it. The first digit of the tactical number identifies the battalion (416th Tank Battalion); the other battalion used tactical numbers starting at 7 as is shown in the plate of the M3L previously.

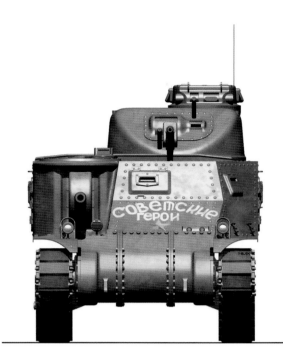

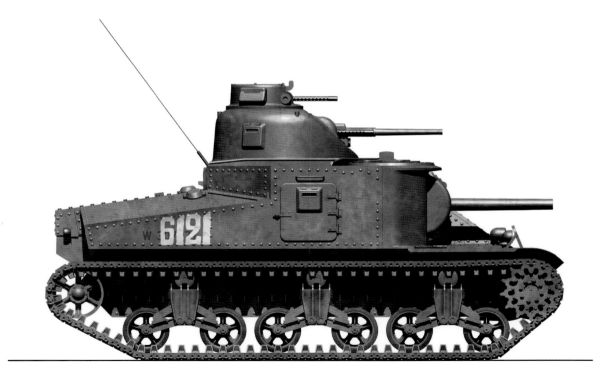

A Matilda lost on the Southern Front during the fighting in July 1942.

COMBAT IN 1942: OPERATION *BLAU*

Lend-Lease tanks were arguably the most important during the First Protocol period when Soviet tank production had been crippled. Much of Soviet industry was in the regions of Russia and Ukraine that were threatened or overrun by the Wehrmacht in 1941. The tank industry was in turmoil and the major plants in Leningrad and Kharkov were moved to the safety of the Urals. The chaos severely curtailed tank production. For example, a July 20, 1941 decree on the manufacture of 10,000 T-60 light tanks in the second half of 1941 saw the production of only 1,830 T-40 and T-60 light tanks. A similar plan to build 710 T-34 tanks at the Krasnoe Sormovo plant in Gorkiy resulted in the construction of only 161 in the second half of 1941. The situation in early 1942 improved somewhat, but production remained dominated by the cheap T-60 and T-70 light tanks. So, in the first half of 1942, 5,100 light tanks were manufactured which constituted 46 percent of overall tank production while only 4,414 T-34 and 1,663 KV tanks were built. At the start of July 1942, the Red Army had 13,500 tanks of which 2,200 (16 percent) were Lend-Lease tanks, roughly half British/Canadian and half American. At this point, Lend-Lease tanks were a higher proportion of the Soviet tank force than at any later period in the war.

Following the failure of the gargantuan mechanized corps in the 1941 fighting, the Red Army tank force reorganized its units into smaller brigades, regiments, and battalions. The brigades were generally used for tank missions at corps level while the regiments and battalions were generally assigned to the infantry support mission. The brigades at this time typically included two tank battalions, and so had about 40 tanks, while battalions typically had about 20 tanks. In the spring of 1942, the Red Army realized it needed larger, divisional-size tank formations which were called tank corps (tankoviy korpus). In spite of the name, they were closer to a Panzer division in strength, usually with three brigades, each with two tank battalions. These saw their combat debut in the first half of 1942 in response to the German drive towards Stalingrad and the Caucasus oil fields, Operation *Blau*.

At least two of the early tank corps were formed primarily with British tanks. The 10th Tank Corps was formed in the Moscow Military District in April 1942 and had two Matilda battalions among its six tank battalions with a total of 60 Matildas. The 11th Tank Corps, formed in the Moscow Military District in May 1942 had four of its six

A Valentine abandoned after its train was bombed during the fighting outside Kharkov in June 1942.

battalions equipped with the Matilda. It was committed as part of the 5th Tank Army during the July 1942 fighting on the Don River. It started the campaign on July 6, 1942 with 88 Matilda tanks of the 181 tanks in the corps. In about ten days of fighting, it lost 51 Matildas, had 22 more under repair and had only 37 still in service. The 5th Tank Army as a whole started with 641 tanks, and lost 341.

The only corps to be equipped entirely with British tanks in 1942 was the 5th Mechanized Corps formed in September–November 1942 in the Moscow Military District. The mechanized corps were similar to the tank corps, but with a higher motor-rifle content. The 5th Mechanized Corps was equipped with Matilda and Valentine tanks. It saw its combat debut in the Stalingrad offensive in December 1942, but was largely destroyed during Manstein's counter-offensive in February 1943. It was rebuilt afterwards, mainly with Valentine tanks, and returned to combat in August 1943 in the Smolensk area. The new 23rd Tank Corps had a heavy American component with two battalions of Lend-Lease tanks including 38 M3Ls and three M3Ss among its 128 tanks.

Most Lend-Lease tanks during this period were issued to the small separate tank regiments and tank battalions that were used primarily in the infantry support role. As in

A curious photograph of a pair of M3Ls during training on the North Caucasus Front in October 1942. The crew is still wearing the American padded tankers' helmets which were not often seen in Soviet use. These tanks were delivered with the Thompson sub-machine gun for crew defense.

the case of the neighboring units equipped with Soviet tanks, the rate of attrition was horrifically high with about 15,000 Soviet tanks lost in combat in 1942.

NEW ARRIVALS: THE CHURCHILL INFANTRY TANK

Although the Soviet mission in Britain expressed interest in the Churchill infantry tank in 1941, British authorities were concerned about its early mechanical problems and declined to ship any. In addition, the decision to up-arm the type to the 6-pdr as well as Soviet disdain for the 2-pdr led to further delays. The first 25 Churchills were shipped to the Soviet Union in May 1942; of the first 30 sent through by June 30, 20 were sunk en route delaying the entry of the type into Soviet service. One of the early arrivals was sent to Kubinka for trials. The report from the proving ground concluded that "The armor and armament of the English heavy tank MK.4 Churchill is sufficient to fight any German tank. The MK.4 is unrefined both from a design and production standpoint. When used in the field, it will require frequent repairs and replacement of parts and entire sub-assemblies."

The Churchill, usually called the MK.4 in Soviet service, was not especially popular and was not shipped in large numbers with only 258 arriving. They were classified as a heavy tank, and so assigned eventually to separate

E

CHURCHILL III, 49TH SEPARATE GUARDS BREAKTHROUGH HEAVY TANK REGIMENT, LENINGRAD FRONT, FEBRUARY 1944

This particular unit had been formed in October 1942 from the previous 168th Tank Brigade at Gorkiy receiving new Churchill tanks. This Churchill III was delivered in the usual SCC No. 2 Brown camouflage paint, but the unit has over-painted it with white-wash. Instead of giving the tank an overall coat of white, bands of the base brown color have been left to break up the camouflage. The markings consist of a two-digit tactical number and the name Aleksandr Nevskiy below this. Nevskiy was the legendary prince who had defeated the Teutonic Knights in 1242 at Lake Peipus, no doubt well known during the war from the 1938 film by Sergei Eisenstein. The Guards insignia is painted on both sides of the turret front.

A pair of Churchill tanks of the Guards 26th Heavy Breakthrough Tank Regiment on the streets of Vyborg during the fighting with Finland in the summer of 1944. At this point, the regiment only had six Churchill tanks and the regiment was filled out using 31 KV-1S heavy tanks.

Guards breakthrough tank regiments which were basically infantry support units. These regiments were committed to combat starting in the early winter of 1942–43 on the Don Front, and later to the Leningrad and Volkhov fronts. Some Churchills survived into 1944. For example, the mixed 82nd Tank Regiment used Churchills alongside KV-1S tanks during the fighting in Estonia in the summer of 1944.

The Churchill had an unexpected influence on future Soviet tanks. Soviet tank designers were impressed by the roof-mounted periscope used on the Churchill, since it was simple but offered good vision. This periscope was based on the pre-war Polish Gerlach periscope used on the 7TP light tank. Although the Red Army had captured some 7TPs in 1939, this feature was largely overlooked at the time. In 1943, the Soviet designers decided to copy the British design for their new tank periscope, which was called the MK-4 based on the Churchill's usual Russian designation. This became a standard feature on later World War II tank designs such as the T-34-85 and IS-2 tanks, as well as on many post-war tanks and armored vehicles.

THE AMERICAN TANK CONUNDRUM

The Second Protocol covering July 1942 to June 1943 envisioned a substantial increase in British and American aid to the Soviet Union with Britain pledging 3,000 tanks and the United States pledging 7,000, for a grand total of 10,000 tanks. These totals included undelivered tanks from the previous protocol. The Second Protocol ran into substantial delivery problems due to German attacks on the Arctic convoys and there was a backlog of 2,583 tanks unshipped as of February 1943.

During the period covered by the Second Protocol, there was considerable internal debate in Moscow regarding the desirability of ordering more American tanks. As mentioned earlier, the head of the Soviet tank industry, Vyacheslav Malyshev, had condemned the M3L and M3S in May 1942 and recommended acquiring more American trucks instead. Gen Maj A. I. Belyaev, the head of the Soviet Purchasing Committee in Washington D.C., was sent a detailed list of complaints about the American tanks from Moscow and forwarded this to Brig Gen John Christmas, the head of the US Tank and Automotive Center, in August 1942. By the time the list had arrived, it was largely irrelevant since many of the technical issues raised in the report had either been corrected or the tank type was no longer in production.

Technical interchanges between the Soviet and American tank industries had little influence and were not as productive as the friendly and cooperative relationship between the US and Britain. The Soviet Union largely refused to exchange any technical details about its own tanks with the United States. British officials in Moscow finally convinced the Soviet government to ship examples of Soviet tanks to the US and Britain as a goodwill gesture, and single samples of the T-34 medium tank and KV-1 heavy tank were sent to both countries in late 1942. Soviet officers visited the main US tank proving ground at Aberdeen, Maryland on numerous occasions, but their frequent criticisms of US tank designs were viewed with growing irritation by US officials, since they were unwilling to share any information about Soviet tank design.

In October 1942, the US war correspondent Leland Stowe published a series of syndicated newspaper articles based on his travels to the Russian Front near Rzhev. They were very critical of the M3S tank stating that it was inferior to British and Soviet tanks. In response to the public controversy stirred up by these articles, Gen Belyaev wrote again to Brig Gen Christmas hoping to calm down the controversy:

> Except for certain disadvantages which I mentioned in my letter of August 11th, 1942, the American made tanks have advantages which I would like to stress: 1.) Good performance of transmission and engine assembly. 2.) Considerable firing power. 3.) Satisfactory armored protection of turret and front part of the bow of the Medium Tank M3. 4.) Sufficient cruising range of the Medium Tank. 5.) Satisfactory Visibility. 6.) Great mobility and good maneuverability of Light Tank M3. It is well known that it is impossible to design a universal vehicle sufficient to meet every condition, and each one of the existing tank models possess some good features and disadvantages. It would not be right to come to a conclusion that American made tanks are not effective in our country.

Another detailed list of complaints about the American tanks was forwarded to the US Army headquarters in Washington D.C. in November 1942 via Col Philip Faymonville, the former military attaché to the USSR who had been appointed by Roosevelt to manage Lend-Lease affairs in Moscow. As was the case of the August 1942 letter from the Soviet Purchasing Commission, many of the issues were no longer relevant due to the rapidity of production changes in the US tank industry in 1942.

Disagreements over the desirability of ordering more Lend-Lease American tanks roiled the Soviet government. The headquarters of the Red Army Armored and Mechanized Forces (BTiMV-KA: *Bronetankoviy i Mekhanizirovannoy Voisk Krasnoy Armii*) was asked its assessment of American tanks in preparation for the negotiations for the Third Protocol. On January 12, 1943, assistant chiefs Generals Nikolai I. Biryukov and Boris M. Korobkov responded to the commissar for foreign trade Anastas Mikoyan, reiterating the existing complaints about the M3L and M3S. A small number of the new M4A2 medium tanks had arrived in late 1942, but the only data on these was a draft Kubinka report that included a complaint about the engine fuel injectors.

By this time, Soviet tank production had been restored in the Urals and there was no longer the desperate need for foreign tanks that had been the case in 1941–42. As a result, BTiMV recommended that, instead of more American tanks, M2 and

Nearly all Shermans sent to Russia were the diesel-powered M4A2. A pair of the M4A4s that were sent were these early production types with direct-vision devices on the drivers' hoods. This particular tank was tested at the NIIBT Poligon at Kubinka, and is fitted with a non-standard counterweight on the gun mantlet.

M3 half-tracks be substituted along with specialized tank repair equipment. In the event, Mikoyan heard from other officials, such as tank industry chief Malyshev, who were especially keen on more American trucks. Malyshev had managed to restore Soviet tank production by using assets from the automotive industry, and American trucks would help to cover this gap.

As a result of these discussions, the Soviet delegation during negotiations for the Third Protocol in the early spring of 1943 indicated that it was no longer interested in American tanks. Instead, it wanted many more US trucks under the Third Protocol. The Soviet delegation also suggested cancelling existing US commitments for tanks from the Second Protocol and using the limited shipping capacity to deliver more trucks. This was mutually satisfactory to the Soviet and US delegations, because the US Army was completing extensive truck assembly facilities in Iran which would permit delivery around the bottleneck of the Arctic convoys.

In the event, tank deliveries under the Third Protocol did not turn out as originally planned. In late 1942, British and American officials had concluded the Week–Somervell Agreement which attempted to balance British Lend-Lease requirements with British production plans. The US side had recommended that Britain cut back on planned tank production in favor of standardizing on the M4 Sherman, and in return promised 10,000 Sherman tanks under the agreement. However, the tank production cut-backs in Britain combined with Soviet rejection of all of the existing British tank types such as the Centaur, Cromwell, and Churchill, meant that Britain essentially had no tanks to ship to the Soviet Union. Valentine production was ramping down, and although all 1943 production would be directed to the Soviet Union, it would not reach the obligation for 3,000 tanks. Eventually, the US side offered to substitute 2,000 M4A2 Sherman tanks for the remaining part of the British obligation. The Soviet delegation later agreed, re-opening American Lend-Lease tank deliveries.

THE 1943 CAMPAIGN

By 1943, Lend-Lease tanks were in widespread use in the Red Army. The pattern of deployment remained very uneven with the majority of units tending to be composed of either Soviet types or Lend-Lease types, but there were still many units of mixed Soviet/Lend-Lease compositions. The German *Fremde Heere Ost* (FHO: Enemy Armies East) intelligence service estimated Soviet tank unit composition in their periodic assessments as shown in the accompanying chart. Of the units where the composition was identified, about 71 percent were of homogenous Soviet composition, 13 percent Lend-Lease, and 16 percent mixed.

One of the 33 M3L tanks of the 563rd Separate Tank Battalion, that attempted to re-capture the Black Sea port of Novorossiysk by an amphibious landing at Ozereika Bay the night of February 3/4, 1943.

Composition of Soviet Tank Units in 1943					
	Soviet	Lend-Lease	Mixed	Unknown	Total
March 7, 1943					
Tank Brigades	74	13	21	68	176
Tank Regiments	25	2	0	51	78
Tank Battalions	5	3	0	15	23
June 3, 1943					
Tank Brigades	96	21	34	105	256
Tank Regiments	28	5	0	59	92
Tank Battalions	7	4	0	34	45
October 5, 1943					
Tank Brigades	62	9	20	40	131
Tank Regiments	63	9	9	50	131
Tank Battalions	3	–	1	2	6

With regard to the types of Lend-Lease tanks in service in 1943, the three most common types were the Valentine, the M3L light tank and the M3S medium tank. This composition changed as the year went on, with a large surge of Canadian Valentine tanks arriving during the year. A small batch of five M5A1 light tanks was delivered in 1943, but the Red Army showed no interest at all in the type, preferring to use the Valentine for its light scout tank and requesting expanded delivery of the M4A2 Sherman tanks from the United States. The British first displayed the new Cromwell tank to the Soviet liaison team in Britain in November 1942, but the Soviet tank specialists thought that the design was half-baked at the time. There was a brief revival of interest in April 1943, but in the end the British War Office suggested that they transfer M4A2 Sherman III tanks from their Lend-Lease allotment as mentioned earlier.

An M3S of the 193rd Tank Regiment during the fighting on the northern side of the Kursk salient. Like many of the separate infantry support units, this regiment had a large number of its tanks dug in and camouflaged. The M3S was not especially well suited to this tactic, since only its upper 37mm gun cleared the dugout.

At the start of the Battle of Kursk, there were a total of 325 Lend-Lease tanks assigned to the Central and Voronezh fronts, amounting to about 12 percent of the total force of tanks and assault guns. The American types included 150 M3S medium tanks, 77 M3L light tanks, and 38 M4A2 medium tanks. British and Canadian tanks included 50 Valentines, 42 Churchills, and 18 Matildas. The Lend-Lease tanks on the Central Front, covering the northern Orel flank of the Kursk salient, consisted mostly of American types. This included the 45th Tank Regiment (30 M3Ss, 9 M3Ls), the 193rd Tank Regiment (55 M3Ss, 3 M3Ls) and the 229th Tank Regiment (38 M4A2s). There were 19 British Lend-Lease tanks in the 19th Tank Corps, probably Valentines. This pattern was largely repeated on the Voronezh Front which had one tank brigade (192nd) and two tanks regiments (230th, 245th) with a total of 65 M3S and 68 M3L tanks. The only separate tank unit with British/Canadian types on this front was the 201st Tank Brigade with 18 Matildas and 31 Valentines. The 2nd and 5th Guards Tank Corps, in front reserve, each had a heavy breakthrough tank regiment with 21 Churchills each. When the 5th Guards Tank Army intervened around Prokhorovka in the

A Churchill of the 10th Guards Heavy Breakthrough Regiment attached to the 23rd Tank Corps of the 1st Tank Army, knocked out on the Voronezh Front on the southern shoulder of the Kursk salient on July 21, 1943.

A Churchill of the Guards 36th Heavy Breakthrough Tank Regiment of the 18th Tank Corps of the Voronezh Front passes a knocked out Sd.Kfz.232 heavy armored car of the 7.Panzer-Division in the wake of the fighting on the southern side of the Kursk salient in August 1943. This unit used the slogan "Za radyansku Ukrainu" (For Soviet Ukraine) on the side of the tank turrets.

middle of July, its units were made up mainly of Soviet types, but the 18th Tank Corps had the 36th Guards Heavy Breakthrough Tank Regiment attached that included 21 Churchills.

Soviet Tank and Assault Gun Strength, Kursk Campaign, July 1943		
	Soviet Tanks and Assault Guns	Lend-Lease Tanks
Central Front		
13th Army	227	–
48th Army	49	132
60th Army	66	–
65th Army	127	–
70th Army	117	–
2nd Tank Army	447	–
Front Reserves	374	19
Voronezh Front		
6th Guards Army	72	78
7th Guards Army	194	49
38th Army	81	55
40th Army	141	–
1st Tank Army	587	–
Front Reserves	368	42
Sub-Total	*2,850*	*375*
5th Guards Tank Army	645	21
Total	*3,495*	*396*

LEFT
Matilda CS tanks of the 5th Mechanized Corps of the 68th Army on the Southwestern Front in the autumn of 1943.

RIGHT
A Valentine IX armed the 6-pdr, knocked out in the fighting in the winter of 1943.

An M4A2 (76mm) of the 219th Tank Brigade, 1st Guards Mechanized Corps in Berlin in May 1945.

of 3,000 M4A2s (76mm) to the Soviet Union. Due to the shortfalls in the Third Protocol deliveries, a batch of M4A2s (76mm) manufactured in May–June 1944 was substituted. The M4A2 (76mm) began arriving in the Soviet Union in late 1944 and the first known combat use was in December 1944 with the 9th Guards Mechanized Corps of the 6th Guards Tank Army.

In January 1945, M4A2 (76mm) production shifted from the existing VVS (vertical volute suspension) to the improved HVSS (horizontal volute suspension system). Of the 2,073 M4A2s (76mm) sent to the Soviet Union, about 460 were the late style with HVSS. Due to the end of the war in Europe, the Fourth Protocol was not entirely implemented as Lend-Lease drew to a close. So far as is known, none of the late HVSS type was deployed in combat in the European theater, as much of this delivery took place through the Pacific ports. Tank deliveries continued well after May 1945 under the

An M4A2 (76mm) of the 64th Guards Tank Regiment, 8th Guards Mechanized Corps near Grabow, Germany on May 3, 1945. The slogan on the side is "Vpered k pobede!" (Forward to Victory).

Some of the final production M4A2s (76mm) with the new HVSS suspension were delivered in the final batches of Shermans in 1945. It is not known whether any of this version saw combat in Europe, but some may have seen action in the *August Storm* operation against the Japanese in Manchuria in 1945. As many as 460 Shermans with HVSS were delivered to the Soviet Union in 1945.

"Milepost" agreement that anticipated Soviet entry into the war against Japan later in 1945. Some HVSS tanks were deployed with the 6th Guards Tank Army in the summer of 1945, but it is unclear whether they took part in the August 1945 *August Storm* offensive against Japan in Manchuria.

Red Army Tanks in the Soviet Far East, August 5, 1945			
	Ready	In Repair	Total
M4A2	250	–	250
Valentine	78	3	81
M3L	–	1	1
M3S	–	1	1
Soviet types	4,513	702	5,215
Total tanks	4,841	707	5,548

TANK DESTROYERS

The British Army had requested that US Army Ordnance develop a tank destroyer on the M3 half-track armed with the 6-pdr gun, and a pilot was ordered in April 1942 as the T48 57mm GMC (Gun Motor Carriage). It entered production in December 1942 and 962 were built by the time production ceased in May 1943. By this time, the British Army regarded the 6-pdr as inadequate for the antitank role. The vehicles were offered to the Red Army, which took 650 of them. Britain received 30 and, along with the remaining 282 vehicles in American hands, they were rebuilt as ordinary half-tracks. As a result, the T48 was the only British or American armored fighting vehicle to be used in combat exclusively by the Red Army. The Red Army re-designated them as SU-57 and formed them into special independent tank destroyer brigades consisting of three

Almost all of the production run of the T48 57mm Gun Motor Carriage was sent to the Red Army. This is an example in a tank destroyer brigade in Prague in May 1945.

battalions with a total of 60 SU-57s each. The first of these brigades to see combat was the 16th Separate Tank Destroyer Brigade which went into action during the Dnepr River offensive in Ukraine in August 1943. The 19th Brigade fought during the Baranow bridgehead battles in Poland in August 1944, and some of these units took part in the Berlin campaign and Prague campaign in April–May 1945. The SU-57 was also used in separate motorcycle battalions, providing welcome firepower to these reconnaissance units. The Soviets later turned over 15 of these to the Polish People's Army where they were employed by the 7th Self-propelled Artillery Battery during the fighting in Poland and Germany in 1944–45.

The Red Army also accepted 52 M10 3in GMC tank destroyers. It is unclear why such a small number was ordered. They were used to form two self-propelled artillery regiments (SAP: *Samokhodno-artilleriyskiy pol*). The 1223rd SAP Regiment served with the 29th Tank Corps of the 5th Guards Tank Army, 3rd Belorussian Front in the fighting in 1944–45 in Belarus, the Baltic States, and East Prussia. The 1239th SAP Regiment served with the 16th Tank Corps (later 9th Guards Tank Corps) of the 2nd Tank Army, 1st Belarussian Front and served in the 1944–45 campaigns in Belarus and Poland. It was subsequently re-designated as the 387th Guards SAP Regiment due to its superior combat performance. The Red Army also received a few M18 76mm GMCs, but did not particularly like the type due to its very thin armor.

LIGHT ARMORED VEHICLES

The Red Army showed very little interest in British or American armored cars. At least three AEC MK.II heavy armored cars were delivered in 1943, but tests at Kubinka were very critical of the design.

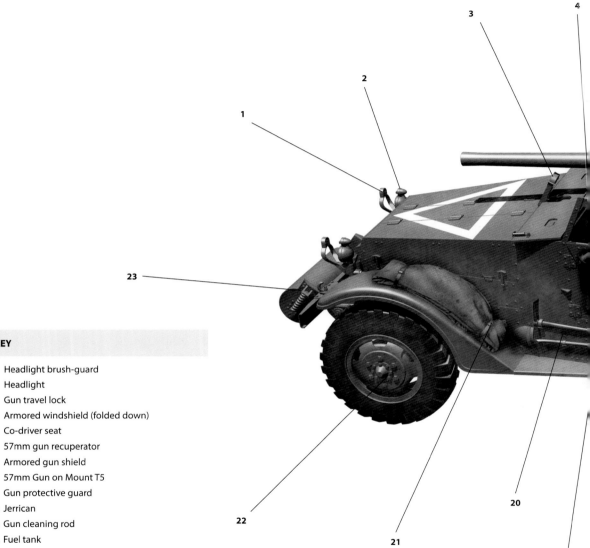

KEY

1. Headlight brush-guard
2. Headlight
3. Gun travel lock
4. Armored windshield (folded down)
5. Co-driver seat
6. 57mm gun recuperator
7. Armored gun shield
8. 57mm Gun on Mount T5
9. Gun protective guard
10. Jerrican
11. Gun cleaning rod
12. Fuel tank
13. External stowage bin
14. Ammunition ready rack (20-round top bin)
15. Idler wheel
16. Main suspension bogie
17. Drive sprocket
18. Driver's seat
19. Steering wheel and driver's controls
20. Vehicle tools
21. Vehicle tarp
22. Driven front wheels
23. Roller bumper

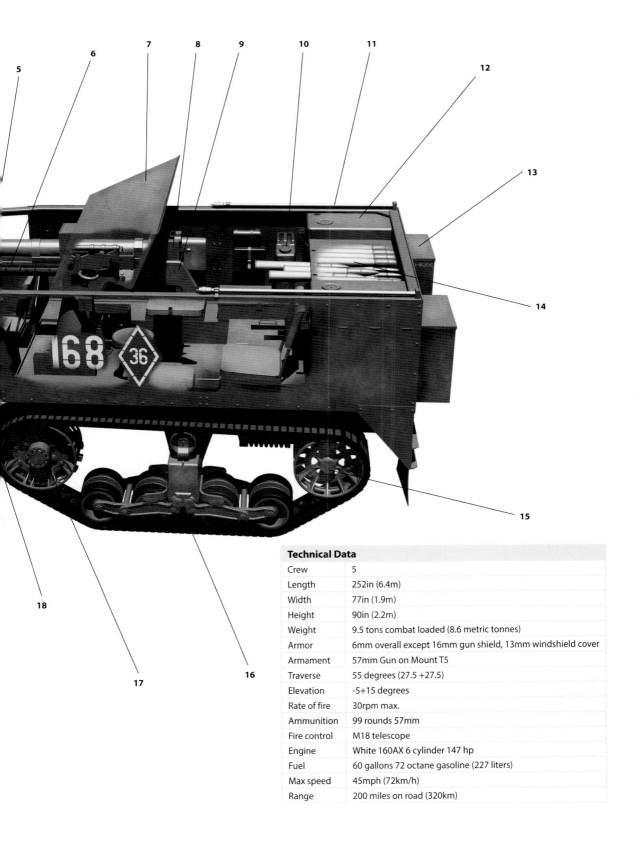

Technical Data	
Crew	5
Length	252in (6.4m)
Width	77in (1.9m)
Height	90in (2.2m)
Weight	9.5 tons combat loaded (8.6 metric tonnes)
Armor	6mm overall except 16mm gun shield, 13mm windshield cover
Armament	57mm Gun on Mount T5
Traverse	55 degrees (27.5 +27.5)
Elevation	-5+15 degrees
Rate of fire	30rpm max.
Ammunition	99 rounds 57mm
Fire control	M18 telescope
Engine	White 160AX 6 cylinder 147 hp
Fuel	60 gallons 72 octane gasoline (227 liters)
Max speed	45mph (72km/h)
Range	200 miles on road (320km)

The Universal Carrier was widely used in Red Army reconnaissance battalions. These units sometimes kept the Lend-Lease weapons supplied with the vehicle, in this case, the Boys antitank rifle in the front and the Bren light machine gun with the gunner in the rear compartment.

Because of the Soviet Union's rough road network, the Red Army was more interested in tracked vehicles that offered better cross-country performance. The first of these was the British Universal Carrier. These were among the earliest British types delivered, with 330 arriving in 1941. Eventually, some 2,360 were shipped, including 1,348 from Canada, of which 2,008 arrived. A further 103 of the Carrier, "Tracked, Starting and Charging" based on the Loyd Carrier, were also delivered as well as 96 of the American T16 version. The Universal Carrier was widely used as a utility vehicle in the headquarters of tank and mechanized units with two or three attached to each company. They were also widely used by Red

Soviet allied armies including the Polish LWP received some Lend-Lease equipment via the Soviet Union such as this Universal Carrier that served with the 1 *Korpus pancery* (1st Tank Corps) in 1945.

An M3A1 scout car of the 3rd Guards Tank Corps on the 2nd Belorussian Front in April 1945.

Army reconnaissance units, such as the separate reconnaissance companies (*otdelniy razvedyvatelniy rot*).

The United States shipped a variety of light armored vehicles, of which the M3A1 scout car was by far the most popular. A total of 3,340 of these were shipped to the Red Army, of which 3,034 were delivered. These were used, much like the Universal Carrier, as utility vehicles in armored units and especially for reconnaissance applications. In later years, the Red Army also ordered the armored half-tracks, and a total of 404 M2/M3 half-tracks were delivered and a further 420 of the International Harvester version, the M5/M9.

Although the Red Army showed very little interest in US antiaircraft guns, there was more interest in mobile antiaircraft guns based on the armored half-tracks. The most popular of these was the M17 multiple machine-gun motor carriage (MMMC) with 1,000 delivered. This was fitted with an electrically operated quad .50cal machine gun turret in the rear-bed of an M5 half-track. These were used primarily for the mobile defense of tank and mechanized corps. A further 100 of the M15 multiple gun motor carriages (MGMC) were also delivered. These were a 37mm automatic cannon with two co-axial .50cal machine guns in a turret on the rear of an M3 half-track. Very little detail of the use of the M15 by the Red Army has emerged.

The Red Army also obtained at least two LVT-2 amphibious tractors (amtracs). It wanted to order the LVT(A)1 amphibious tank, but for unknown reasons, none was ever delivered.

An M17 Multiple Machine-Gun Motor Carriage (MMMC) armed with four .50cal machine guns in Prague in May 1945. This antiaircraft half-track was essentially similar to the M16 MMMC used by the US Army, but fitted on the International Harvester M5/M9 half-track which had the rounded rear corners of the superstructure as seen here.

At least one Churchill Crocodile flame-thrower tank was delivered to the Soviet Union in 1944 and it is seen here at the NIIBT Poligon at Kubinka during trials.

RARITIES AND LATE ARRIVALS

A variety of tanks and specialized tank derivatives were shipped to the Soviet Union for technical evaluation. In April 1943, three Churchill Crocodile flame-thrower tanks, and three Sherman Crab flail anti-mine tanks were sent to the Soviet Union. Britain offered bridgelayers based on the Covenanter or Valentine, and the Red Army ordered ten Valentine Scissors Bridgelayer tanks.

Under the Fourth Protocol that covered from July 1, 1944 to June 30, 1945, Britain sent no significant shipments of tanks to the USSR except for small trials batches, and the M4A2 became the staple of the Lend-Lease program. By this time, Valentine production had ended in both Britain and Canada, the Red Army wasn't keen on the Churchill infantry tank or the Centaur and Cromwell cruiser tanks. In 1944, the Soviet mission in Britain asked the War Office what it considered to be the best British-manufactured tank.

Ten Valentine Scissors Bridgelayers were delivered to the Soviet Union in 1944 where they were designated as MK.3M (M= *mostoukladchik*; bridgelayer). It is not known if they were ever issued to combat units.

It recommended the Cromwell, and so a test batch of six Cromwell IVs arrived in Baku, Azerbaijan in August 1944. Tests began in the autumn of 1944 at Kubinka. The tests concluded that the Cromwell was inferior to the M4A2 Sherman in all respects except for road speed. The comparison was even worse if the Cromwell was measured against the newer M4A2 (76mm) that was beginning to arrive in the USSR. As a result, the Red Army rejected any orders of the type. At least one Comet tank was delivered later.

The United States sent a few tanks late in the war for trials including the M24 Chaffee light tank and the T26E3 (M26) Pershing tank.

FINAL ASSESSMENT

Assessing the impact of Lend-Lease aid to the Soviet Union in World War II is clouded by the Cold War controversies that erupted about the subject. The Western perspective was that Lend-Lease was a "lifesaver" and a critical element in the eventual Soviet victory. The Soviet viewpoint was that Lend-Lease aid was minor and inconsequential. Information about Lend-Lease was heavily censored in the Soviet Union until the 1991 collapse of the USSR.

US aid to the Soviet Union totaled $10.8 billion of which $5.5 billion was military aid from the US War Department. The remainder was industrial and commercial products including food, fuel, raw materials, and machine tools. Tanks and other combat vehicles were only a small portion of US aid totaling $618.1 million, or about 11 percent of military aid or about six percent of overall aid. This was in no small measure due to Soviet decisions about aid. Soviet disdain for US tanks, especially in the early war years, led to reduced levels of tank delivery. In contrast, the Red Army's need for American trucks meant that far more aid was provided in this category, totaling some $1.14 billion or about 20 percent of total military aid. It is also worth noting that the cost of the infrastructure for delivering this aid was quite considerable, for example some $11 billion being spent on the creation of the Persian Gulf facilities and $53 billion on the Alaska–Siberia route.

British aid totaled some £420 million consisting of £308 million in military aid and £112 million in raw materials and industrial aid. At the Bretton Woods fixed exchange rate, this translates to $1.7 billion in total and $1.2 billion in military aid. Canada provided 1,388 tanks of the 5,218 sent to the Soviet Union, or about a quarter of the British total.

Soviet tank production in World War II was about 85,890 plus a further 21,475 assault guns. The US and Britain shipped 11,663 tanks of which 10,419 arrived, or equivalent to about 13 percent of the Soviet tank force during the war. A less apparent contribution was in the form of machine tools, raw material, and alloys. The US provided the USSR with about 60 percent of its wartime aluminum supply, an essential ingredient in every T-34, KV, and IS-2 engine.

Lend-Lease aid in the form of military trucks was far more significant than tanks. As mentioned earlier, in 1943 the Soviet delegations in the Lend-Lease negotiations cut back the supply of US tanks in exchange for larger shipments of trucks. Moscow selected items for Lend-Lease to cover gaps in its own military industrial capability. Tanks were important in 1941–42 after the disruption of the tank industry by the German invasion but, once

An M3L of the 23rd Guards Tank Brigade of the Western Front in Belgorod in February 1943 with a T-34 behind. This is from the fourth production series with the interim D58101 turret.

the tank industry was restored in 1942–43, Soviet needs for Lend-Lease tanks declined. The Soviet requirement for cross-country trucks was modest in 1941–42 when the Red Army was on the defensive, but Soviet needs for military trucks increased in 1943–44 as the Red Army shifted to the offensive and required greater mobility. The Soviet tank industry had been reconstructed partially by using resources out of the automotive industry, leading to a significant drop in military truck production during the war years. Lend-Lease aid filled this gap. The US provided 501,660 military vehicles to the USSR including 77,972 ¼-ton Jeeps, 151,053 1½-ton trucks, and 200,662 2½-ton trucks; British shipments were far smaller totaling 4,343 trucks and 1,721 motorcycles. Domestic Soviet production during the war was 342,624 vehicles of all types for both civil and military use. The Red Army vehicle park at the end of the war in May 1945 was 640,821 vehicles of which 62 percent was of domestic production, 31 percent Lend-Lease, and the remainder captured German vehicles. Lend-Lease truck supplies indirectly assisted Soviet tank production, since it freed up the resources of the Soviet automotive industry to shift towards armored vehicle production.

The Lend-Lease truck supply was more important in terms of capability than simply in terms of raw numbers. At the beginning of July 1944, the Red Army had received 284,678 new vehicles of which 58 percent were Lend-Lease. Not only did Lend-Lease vehicles represent the majority of new vehicles in Red Army service, they were by far the most important in motorizing the Red Army in time for the 1944 offensives. About 144,000 trucks and military vehicles were delivered by Lend-Lease from January 1943 to June 1944 as the Red Army began to shift to the offensive. Not only did they come at a critical time, but the quality of the equipment was significantly better than domestic Soviet production. The Red Army was still heavily dependent on the GAZ-AA and its variants and the ZiS-5 truck and its variants which were both license-built copies of early 1930s American commercial trucks. These had very poor cross-country capability. In contrast, the Lend-Lease deliveries include types such as the Jeep and 2½-ton Studebaker US6 that were modern military trucks with good cross-country capability. The Red Army of 1944–45 depended primarily on domestic tanks such as the T-34 and IS-2, but the motorization of its combat units depended on Lend-Lease trucks.

Red Army Tank and Assault Guns, June 3, 1945

	At the front	In reserve	In districts*	In repair	Total
Lend-Lease light tanks	207	109	295	303	914
SU-57	250	66	10	14	340
Lend-Lease medium tanks	877	219	275	446	1,817
Soviet light tanks	300	269	2,006	1,108	3,683
Soviet medium, heavy tanks and assault guns	10,382	2,302	2,494	3,065	18,243
Total	12,016	2,965	5,080	4,936	24,997

These are mainly tanks in training units or new units being formed.

Obsolete Lend-Lease Tanks in Red Army, May 20, 1945

	In service	In repair/training units	Total
Matilda	40	182	222
Churchill	7	67	74
M3L	126	77	203
M3S	29	42	71

Lend-Lease Tank & AFV Deliveries to the Soviet Union 1941–45

	1941	1942	1943	1944	1945	Sent*	Delivered*
Matilda II	145	626	147	–	–	932	918
Valentine	216	959	1,776	381	–	3,275	3,332
Churchill	–	84	179	–	–	258	263
Cromwell	–	–	–	6	–	6	6
Tetrarch	–	20	–	–	–	20	20
M3 Stuart	–	977	255	–	–	1,676	1,232
M5A1 Stuart	–	–	5	–	–	5	5
M24 Chafee	–	–	–	–	2	2	2
M3 Lee	–	812	164	–	–	1,386	976
M4A2 Sherman	–	36	469	2,345	814	4,102	3,664
M26 Pershing	–	–	–	–	1	1	1
M10 3in GMC	–	–	–	52	–	52	52
M18 76mm GMC	–	–	5	–	–	5	5
T48 57mm GMC	–	–	241	409	–	650	650
M31 ARV	–	–	41	86	–	115	127
Total	361	3,514	3,282	3,279	817	12,485	11,253

"Delivered" counts vehicles received by the USSR. "Sent" includes those dispatched; some were sunk in transit by sea.

Tanks and AFVs Delivered to the Soviet Union from Britain and Canada

	Sent	Sunk	Arrived
Tetrarch	20	–	20
Matilda III	113	–	113
Matilda IV	915	221	694
Matilda IVCS	156	31	125
Valentine II	161	25	136
Valentine III	346	–	346
Valentine IV	570	71	449
Valentine V	340	113	227
Valentine VII	1,388	180	1,208
Valentine IX	836	18	818
Valentine X	74	8	66
Churchill II	45	19	26
Churchill III	151	24	127
Churchill IV	105	–	105
Cromwell IV	6	–	6
Valentine Bridgelayer	25	–	25
Total	5,251	710	4,491

US Tank and AFV Lend-Lease Deliveries

	Sent	Sunk	Arrived
M3 Light Tank	1,676	443	1,232
M5A1 Light Tank	5	–	5
M24 Light Tank	2	–	2
M3 Medium Tank	1,386	410	976
M4 Medium Tank	4,102	438	3,664
T26E3 Heavy Tank	1	–	1
M10 3-in GMC	52	–	52
M18 76mm GMC	5	–	5
T48 57mm GMC	650	–	650
M15 MGMC	100	–	100
M17 MGMC	1,000	–	1,000
M31 Tank recovery vehicle	130	3	127
M3A1 Scout Car	3,340	228	3,034
M2, M3 half-track	404	–	–
M5 Half-track	420	–	–
T16 Universal Carrier	96	–	–
LVT-2 Amtrac	2	–	–

Note: The Sent and Sunk figures above are taken from US shipment records and the Arrived figures are taken from Russian acceptance records. Any inconsistency in this table is due to discrepancies between the US and Russian archives.

FURTHER READING

There are no monographs on Lend-Lease tanks in English, and few in Russian. The Kolomiets/Moshchanskiy book detailed below provides the story from the Russian perspective. There are a number of English-language histories of Lend-Lease but these tend to look at it from the diplomatic and strategic perspective, usually with little detail about actual weapons delivery.

The Beaumont book on British military aid, listed below, is a rare exception. The historian Alexander Hill has written several articles for the *Journal of Slavic Military Studies* on early British Lend-Lease tank deliveries. There are numerous articles on Lend-Lease Soviet tanks in various Russian magazines including *Tankomaster* and *M-Khobbi*. The collection of the wartime records of GABTU (Main Automotive and Tank Administration) edited by Polonskiy has a number of interesting documents on Lend-Lease.

Much of this book has been researched from archival sources including a range of documents on the US program from the US National Archives and Records Administration in College Park, Maryland. British records that were consulted from the National Archives (formerly Public Records Office) in Kew included the War Office files in WO 32/10521 and WO 193/580. Public Archives of Canada files that were consulted were RG 24, Volume 2626. There are a number of useful internet resources, especially the numerous articles on the subject by Yuri Pasholok on Warspot.ru and there have been English translations of many of these on the ever-intriguing site Archive Awareness (tankarchives.blogspot.com).

Beaumont, Joan, *Comrades in Arms: British Aid to Russia 1941–45*
        (Davis-Poynter: 1980)
Coakley, Robert, and Leighton, Richard, *The War Department: Global Logistics and Strategy 1940–1943* (US Center of Military History: 1995)
Coakley, Robert, and Leighton, Richard, *The War Department: Global Logistics and Strategy 1943–1945* (US Center of Military History: 1989)
Kolomiets, Maksim, and I. Moshchanskiy, *Tanki lend-liza* (Eksprint: 2000)
Loza, Dmitriy, *Commanding the Red Army's Sherman Tanks* (University of Nebraska Press: 1996)
Polonskiy, V. A. et al. (eds), *Glavnoe Avtobronetankoboe Upravlenie: Lyudi, sobytiya, fakti, v documentakh, Vol. 3 (1943–44); Vol. IV (1944–45),* (Russian Defense Ministry: 2006)
Sharp, Charles, *Soviet Order of Battle, Volume XII, Soviet Self-Propelled Artillery and Lend Lease Armor 1941–45* (Nafziger Collection: 1998)
Vail Motter, T. H., *The Middle East Theater: The Perisan Gulf Corridor and Aid to Russia* (Center of Military History: 2000)

INDEX

Figures in **bold** refer to illustrations.